BETWEEN ROOT AND SKY: A COLLECTION OF POEMS
ON LOVE, LOSS AND LONGING

ALICIA M. RODRIGUEZ

Copyright © 2025 Alicia M. Rodriguez

All rights reserved. No part of this publication may be reproduced, distributed, or transmitted in any form or by any means, including photocopying, recording, digital scanning, or other electronic or mechanical methods, without the prior written permission of the publisher, except in the case of brief quotations embodied in critical reviews and certain other non-commercial uses permitted by copyright law. For permission requests, please address Sophia Press.

Published 2025 by Sophia Press

Print ISBN: 978-0-9797958-9-3

E-ISBN: 978-0-9797958-8-6

For information address:

Alicia M. Rodriguez

Sophia Press

www.aliciamrodriguez.com

Book Cover Design by ebooklaunch.com

Company and/or product names that are trade names, logos, trademarks, and/or registered trademarks of third parties are the property of their respective owners and are used in this book for purposes of identification and information only under the Fair Use Doctrine.

NO AI TRAINING: Without in any way limiting the author's and the rights of Sophia Press the publisher, exclusive rights under copyright, any use of this publication to "train" generative artificial intelligence (AI) technologies to generate text is expressly prohibited. The author reserves all rights to license uses of this work for generative AI training and development of machine learning language models.

For more info on Alicia's work and writing and books, scan this QR Code.

*"We belong to both the earth that holds us
and the vastness that calls us home.
In between are the stories of our lives."*

Alicia M. Rodriguez

CONTENTS

Introduction	xi

MOVEMENT ONE
THRESHOLDS

Walk Softly	3
Fall in Love with Someone	5
Love In the Morning	7
There Are Days	9
Love Letters	11
A Thorny Love	13
Secret Lovers	15
Broken Promises	17
Faithless	19
The Flutist	21
Truth	23
Surrender	25
Goodbye In Four Lines	27
If	29
A Christmas Card for Donna	31
One Breath Away	33
Full Moon	35
Wolf	37
Winter	39
Movement	41
Flock	43
Bare	45
The Song Sings Me	47
Praia do Pintadinho -- Portugal	49
Curve	51
Mottled	53
Kludde (my cat)	55
Ripples	57
Nearly	59

A Walk in the Autumn Forest	61
Goodbye Summer	63
Sonora: The Stories of the Desert	65
Draw Your Own Map	67

MOVEMENT TWO
THE UNRAVELING

A Poem for Mina	71
Unforgotten	75
Death	77
Requiem at Christmastime	79
A mi padre	81
A mi padre (English translation)	83
Romeo and Juliet	85
Shadows Before Spring	87
Waiting	91
All the things	93
Whispers in the Walls	95
White Harbor	97
I Died A Thousand Deaths	99
Seduction	101
When I die	103
A Bear in the Forest	105
Battered	107
Context	109
Fear of Falling	111
Memories	113
Song for Ophelia	115
The Latina Washes Her Face	117
Hormones	119
History on the Wall	121
Moving	123
Moving II	125
The Mystery	127

MOVEMENT THREE
RETURNING

Birth of The Mystic	131
Belief	133
God is praying tonight	135
Invitation to Dine	137
A Holy Mist	139
The Dream: Act VI	141
My Quest	143
Shaman's Ceremony	145
Sleepwalker	147
Sculpting the Soul	149
Glimpses of Poems	151
Chance	153
The Place of Words	155
The Silent Ones	157
The Ocean I Sourced From	159
Between Root and Sky	161
NOTES	163
About the Author	165
Follow Alicia on Social Media	167
Also by Alicia M. Rodriguez	169
The End	171

INTRODUCTION

There is a place where we live our entire lives — suspended between what grounds us and what calls us upward into mystery. We are creatures of root and sky, held by earth while longing for flight, shaped by attachment while practicing the art of letting go.

This collection is arranged as a journey, though not the kind that begins at point A and arrives neatly at point B. Life doesn't move in straight lines, and neither do these poems. They spiral, circle back, descend and rise — the way we actually live through love and loss, attachment and letting go.

We begin in **Thresholds** — those ordinary moments when we form our deepest bonds with lovers, children, landscape, and the lineage of women who taught us how to belong. This is the ground beneath our feet, the place where roots take hold. But thresholds are also doorways, and eventually life asks us to walk through them.

The Unraveling is what comes when the ground shifts. Grief arrives. Loneliness settles in. The self we thought we knew begins to dissolve. These poems sit in that dissolution without rushing toward resolution. They honor what it means to stand in the dark, to lose words, to feel the full weight of what falls apart. This section is longer than you might expect for darkness — because that's how it actually is. We don't pass through grief quickly, and the poems respect that truth.

Returning is not about fixing or transcending what came before. It's integration — carrying our losses as carefully as our loves, discovering that the mystic and the ordinary are the same thing, understanding that the roots that anchor us are the foundation for the reaching for our dreams. This section is shorter, quieter. Not because there's less to say, but because after unraveling, we speak more simply. We know what matters.

You don't need to read these poems in order, though the arc is there if you want it. You can enter anywhere — at the threshold, in the unraveling, or in the return. Wherever you are in your own journey, there's a poem here that will meet you.

The poems remember for you what you already know.

With great affection,

Alicia

MOVEMENT ONE
THRESHOLDS

ON LOVE

ON NATURE

WALK SOFTLY

Walk softly, the wind whispered

as leaves crackled under my feet.

Walk firmly, the ground called

as my steps created my path.

Walk gently, sang the birds

as I raised my voice to sing.

Walk forward, she whispered

as I opened my heart to the world.

And the wise one spoke, saying,

as long as you breathe,

as long as you love,

as long as the world calls you forth,

Walk softly,

Walk firmly,

Walk gently,

Always keep walking forward.

FALL IN LOVE WITH SOMEONE

Fall in love with someone who is unafraid of

your darkness,

who doesn't judge your flaws and imperfections,

who stands with you

when your shadow overwhelms you.

Fall in love with the one who dances

with your joy and grief,

offers comfort and pushes limitations,

who loves you when you're strong and

loves you when you're weary.

Fall in love with someone

who stands beside you when

you need a friend,

who stands in front of you to

take a blow,

who stands behind you so

you can lead,

someone to be quiet with or

to be loud with,

someone who is present.

Fall in love with someone

who knows how to love you.

LOVE IN THE MORNING

Wrapped in a cool cotton sheet

and warm wool blanket I find

you

burrowed deep in sleep.

I walk into your dreams

calling you out of the

clouds

to come dance with me

in the morning light.

THERE ARE DAYS

There are days

the immensity

of love in my being

becomes an unbearable burden.

Those days become clouded

with inexplicable grief,

an ocean that has

nowhere to flow,

a dove that cannot

fly.

The pull of the earth

so tight in my chest,

grasping to cure

the longing of

something

unfulfilled yet

filled

too much,

overflowing its boundaries.

Bittersweet.

Delicious.

Exquisite.

Is this what is possible?

This infinite sort of

love that cannot be held

by one heart

or even many?

LOVE LETTERS

You say that I am silent

yet my stillness speaks truth.

My language is a whisper.

The expression of love and hope, even fear,

is carried by the breeze not the storm.

Words cannot hold what fills my heart.

Listen to discover the soul within

and there you will find me.

Read me poetry so that my heart may open.

Write love letters delivered by angels.

Colour my world with paint and rainbows

delighting me with joy.

Play music for me so that my body may speak.

There, you will find me, dancing between the stars

to music no one else may hear

except you.

A THORNY LOVE

Roses in hand she asks me how long I'd been in love.

Red rose for love, white rose for respect, yellow for friendship.

Her question is met with a confused silence.

My hand reaches for red, veers to white but white feels so empty, a

blank nothingness.

What is there but a question hanging in the air?

"They have no thorns," she proclaims proudly, but I know

all roses have thorns at least once,

all love has pain many times over.

"Yellow," I say, playing it safe with my heart.

SECRET LOVERS

In the stillness of night

beside the curving river

they meet as clandestine lovers.

Crickets serenade

fireflies flicker,

stars in the indigo sky.

Only the moon

knows what is spoken.

BROKEN PROMISES

I write down the dates

when we make love

a record of a non-record.

You promised, we agreed

with the mediator that

once a week was time

last time I got into

bed

it was cold and stayed so

I've forgotten

putting passion on back burner

no longer burns bright

dull spark

broken promise I still hold you to

but you don't speak

loud silence on cold nights

broken by TV sports games

we no longer play

lost the rulebook

kept the appointment but

no one showed up

FAITHLESS

He has no faith,

nothing to anchor him

in the chaos.

He is in pain.

I see this.

His eyes do not flash

rainbow colours at my

clumsy humor.

His hands caress me absently,

like petting the dog,

his attention lost in

a maze of thoughts.

His voice speaks

out of tune with the words

as if he'd forgotten

all the soul songs we breathe.

The heaviness he carries

bends him like a reed

overcome with mud and tide.

I am the flow.

I wash his faith in

dirty water,

cleanse him of the

darkness and reveal to him

his divine light.

THE FLUTIST

He played my soul

and I found my wanting

deep in the hollow notes

rising from the slender reed.

Caught unaware I lose my

emotional balance normally

preserved in the jar in the

kitchen perched like a lost

bird on the sill.

The waterfall from the source of being

releases

crashing down on the

calm, clear, cool reflection

of the soul.

I lose my place in heaven.

TRUTH

When you can't hear the answer

sit by the ocean and listen

to the racing waves as their music

crashes against the beach in undulating rhythm.

Walk in the forest and listen to the wind

dancing in the trees whispering their secrets

while the leaves rustle beneath your feet

and the sparrows call lovingly to one another.

Stand alone in the middle of the jungle

and you'll hear the night noises speak their truth

in the immense roar of the jaguar as in

the barely-there song of the tree frog.

If you still cannot hear then go deeper

into the heartbeat within you

until the rhythm of the beat betrays

the secret longing of your heart.

There within this universal symphony

come alive to yourself

as the insistent voice of your soul reveals

its truth hidden within the songs of life.

SURRENDER

I asked the ocean

Teach me about surrender

The way the sand gives way

To the tide

The way the stones fight

For their place on the beach

Only to be swept out to

The unknown sea

To be turned and churned

Returning to the shore

A polished version of themselves.

The ocean replies

Throwing stones at my feet

Sand chafes my legs

Salt burns my eyes

Tears stream down my face

Melting back to the mother womb

Where it all began

Where it all ends

That is the way of life

She speaks wisely

Answering the unanswerable.

GOODBYE IN FOUR LINES

Words arise in my mouth like acid wanting to be spit out.

Any nourishment has long ago been depleted.

My tongue curls around the emptiness.

You should've left long ago I tell myself.

IF

If you had said, yes, when I needed to hear it,

had opened your heart when I needed to feel it,

if you had taken my hand to keep me from falling,

then I would be there.

If you had understood that my silence covered my pain,

if you had listened to my heartbeat when we lay together,

if you had looked into my soul and read its message,

then I would be there.

If the world had room for our joys and our sorrows,

and the touch of your hand was kinder and gentle,

if we had shared the same language and songs,

then I would be there.

But I am not there, and you are not here.

There are no songs to sing, no hand to hold,

if only,

if only I could have stayed,

and you could've loved,

then I would be there.

A CHRISTMAS CARD FOR DONNA

Last night

under the flicker of tiny white lights

adorning the Christmas tree

with presents in red, gold and green

with heavenly music filling the air

my soul stole out from hiding

and escaped into the space

between paper and pen

while I wrote a card

for Donna.

I didn't even see it,

I didn't hear it,

so silent and fluid it was

I never felt it.

I didn't sense it.

Oozing out of the pen

it mixed discretely with the ink

onto the snowy white card

hiding

behind the angel and her trumpet.

When you feel unloved and unlovable

look within and see your own divine light.

Look into your heart, past the mist and

the shadows

to the lovely soul which lies waiting to be

released.

It is kind,

it is generous,

it is loving.

My wish for you is that you allow yourself

to see it too.

And I wrote,

until finished I saw

my soul had written me

a message the only way

it could.

ONE BREATH AWAY

The earth crunches under foot

this morning

soaking in fiery rays

scorches my skin, burning

eyes open

The endless ocean offers itself

to me

wave upon wave crashing

on wide deserted beaches

we arrive

Never knowing which comes first

the falcon

or the gull soaring

only one breath away

from falling

Faith follows a secret path

through brush

scratching my arms, legs

urging me onward blindly

seeking significance

I am one breath away

from death

the ticking of time

that mercilessly urges me

to live.

FULL MOON

The moon glows on the horizon

as gentle cool waters of ocean gather

in deep contemplation while

whales swim in deep shadows and

stars twinkle messages in a velvet moon night.

WOLF

The night winds

howl through the trees

moonlight scatters crystals

on the ground

when next appears

another sound.

With slow gait

and soft landing

slyly a shadow

darts in and out

then pauses

to sing aloud.

He is her lover,

nights when she appears

brilliance

cutting forest canopy

and his voice

for all to hear.

Mystery dwells in the shadows

earth and sky commune

heart songs in the night

the wolf and his lover

the moon.

WINTER

White fluffy snowflakes

melt on her tongue

drifting from the sky

to paint the cold ground.

Making snow angels

in the backyard

squeals of delight

toboggans taking flight.

The child's snowsuit

moist and bulky

enjoys a deep dive

into a blanket of white.

MOVEMENT

This morning, when I woke,

the sun was shining

unaware of fear,

despair,

and

grief.

The way the sunlight

dances on the surface of the pond,

and

the swaying of the Bougainvillea branches

remind me

we can discover harmony in chaos

and

light in darkness

and joy in pain.

FLOCK

Silence is broken by

A cacophony of trumpeting

Voices and the blur

Of feathers in the sky.

The glassy surface of the lake

Becomes the blue

Invitation

For a flock of geese

Pausing on their journey

Home.

BARE

The trees are bare

Standing like skeletons

Against a blanket of white

Their branches remember

The warmth of a summer sun

The sweetness of dew

The lovers sheltering

Under their full canopy

From the pelting rain

Trees

Have long memories of

Seasons and cycles

Birth and death

Knowing wisely

Their time to flourish

Soon returns

THE SONG SINGS ME

The song sings me

a long and plaintive call

carried on the winds

over soft white clouds

and golden horizons

touching the fragrant evergreen

and sleeping meadows

singing its lullaby

to the silence

of the musty woods

while snowflakes gather

on the mountain

and brown moccasined feet

step gingerly over the

moist autumn leaves

following

as the song sings me.

PRAIA DO PINTADINHO
-- PORTUGAL

The fishermen lean precariously on the edge of the cliffs with their

long lines sweeping into the ocean.

The tide comes in hard, and I wonder if I'll drown again, and again and

again.

Always reaching for the depths of my being as the waves surge

threatening to sweep me away.

I dive deep challenging the ocean's dare. The water chills and I feel

the droplets on my skin like shattered glass rubbing against me.

I rise for a breath in the ebb, feeling the pull back into the ocean, dive deeper through the blue hued waters to anchor myself on the sandy

bottom.

I lose my hold tumbling like a pebble as the sand escapes my fingers

dissolving into memories of another ocean, another beach, another woman,

again and again.

CURVE

Her back aches

pulsing like a drum

someone, everyone beats.

She is mother, daughter, sister, wife.

Her spine once strong

curved over by the weight

of a life relinquished to others.

A life she used to own,

a voice she used to know,

silenced by time and surrender

now remembering the woman she was.

Is.

Can be again.

She stands rebellious.

She stands strong.

She stands up.

Feet grounded in the primordial mother.

Eyes to the sky

she reclaims her place

in the world.

MOTTLED

He arrives in a basket

dwarfed in towels

his body shaking.

"We found him on the road,

couldn't leave the little guy,"

she adds apologetically.

I lift him tenderly

this mottled bundle of fur

and nuzzling him I whisper,

"You're safe now. You're home."

KLUDDE (MY CAT)

I didn't know

his name meant demon

I misunderstood the

the word

yet

he cares not about

his moniker

preferring to lead

his furry, black existence

on his own terms

monitoring

a field of green, brown and blue

like an animate statue

perceiving every movement

in the garden with glowing eyes,

round, green glass orbs reflecting light.

I wonder what he sees or

if he is bored with his life or

if indeed he is the

guru I have waited for

to teach me how to be

still.

RIPPLES

The little pebble

flies

over the surface

skipping

drops of water

flying

a race to the other side of

my lake

alas

she tires

one last burst

dropping into blue

believing all is lost

until above her

circles form

round and round

declaring

I was here

over and over

again.

NEARLY

Two roads cross as I navigate the forest.

Shadows dance as evening falls.

Listening to the call of the wild things,

ready to nestle into

dark wombs in trees

or burrows in musky earth.

Follow the wren

or the crow?

What now?

I am lost.

No.

Nearly there.

Wherever I arrive

I must be.

A WALK IN THE AUTUMN FOREST

I hear whispers in the dim hollows

of a forgotten forest

where light barely seeps in,

more like droplets than rays.

"This world is a sorrowful place," they murmur

where musk and damp

smell of death.

Yet from a distance unseen

bird songs arrive

weaving paths of enlightenment

between protruding branches,

insisting stories of rebirth.

Their songs bless me with radical faith

that beyond every dying thing

in this hallowed ground

there exists

the seedling of new life.

It is the only hope I can carry

when the world turns dark.

GOODBYE SUMMER

This morning,

I wore my fluffy robe and warm slippers

when I went outside.

Summer had gone with a whisper in the night

not even a tender goodbye.

I'll miss you, I called out

as I sipped my dark coffee

blowing the steam into the wind

like an offering

to the changing season.

SONORA: THE STORIES OF THE DESERT

The shadows of late afternoon hide

sacred myths in the craggy recesses of the McDowells

as Sonora casts her spell,

resurrecting legends amidst the purple stillness.

Grains of sand speak a testament

to many a hard-lived life of maize and prickly pear,

partings of the ways between the reds and the whites.

As I stand on this rose quartz hill

I grieve Her dying in the midst of tractor roars, adobe

and concrete walls. Yet She feeds Her renegade children,

refusing to surrender.

I look west.

Silence spoken loudly by the Kachinas is carried on

the wings of hawks to Father Sky.

The setting sun like the forgotten
ceremonial birth fires glow to death
ashes. As the blood red sun touches the horizon
I see their eyes staring from the hills and
hear the warrior voices chanting.
My heart beats the leather-skinned drums
and my feet join in the dance of the Sonora.
I mourn that my children will never know what I know
standing here on the burial mound with Mother Earth
hand in hand with the ancients.

DRAW YOUR OWN MAP

I see the light in the darkness,

feel the heat in the cold.

I can touch you from afar.

I'm not who you thought I'd be.

Not who you are.

I am the breeze that caresses

when you fear your grief,

the voice that whispers

in your aloneness.

I am the moment that startles,

the laugh that invites.

I am the arms you crave

when you feel unlovable.

Footprints on a distant shore
I no longer recognize,
testament to a path taken,
a map someone once gave me
to follow.

I am unknown to myself
unknown to you, a fleeting vapour
glimpses of possibility that cannot be
captured.

Give up all things you believe
I am,
you are.
Surrender the toxins in your mind
that keep you up at night.

Embrace the magic of your journey.

MOVEMENT TWO
THE UNRAVELING

ON LONGING

ON LOSS

A POEM FOR MINA

If I could sit with you today

I might confess you made me smile when all I had to offer were

tears.

We might share stories of travels in Spain, forgotten hours on a beach in Hawaii or the first time we got drunk

together.

If I could sit with you, I would ask you to forgive me for my arrogance and selfishness, for those moments you needed me and I wasn't

there.

. . .

If I could sit with you, I'd hold your weathered hand tenderly like you held mine when I felt lost and

alone.

If I could sit with you, I would hug you closely hoping to never let you

go,

yet knowing that releasing you to the moon and stars was the ultimate

act of love.

If I could sit with you just one more moment you would surely wipe the tears from my eyes and tell me to be strong, live joyfully and never be

afraid of life.

Until the day we sit together again I will hold you in my heart with

grace and joy.

Our loved ones never really leave us. They live in our hearts and in the divine connection we share with all that exists, has existed and will exist. No time or space here. Only an infinite web of love. When we understand this, life fills with grace.

UNFORGOTTEN

Your peonies bloomed late this season

after so many years of silence.

I thought they had died to honor you

rebirthed this season as if to say

"I am still here with you,

growing quietly under the earth,

unforgotten by those I loved."

∽

For my mother Mina who loved peonies.

DEATH

Your life flows like

an unstoppable river rushing,

leaving sweet memory drops

in its wake while

the inevitable tide

reaches giant proportions

to overwhelm your ancient

bones.

Where once was a warrior

of strong voice,

a soft cry emitted

with precious few

breath moments.

No glisten in your eye

now shrouded by the

mist of death.

I watch helplessly on the shore

as you, my dear friend, are

carried away.

I try to stay the flow but

you disappear over the falls.

I stand on the river edge

weeping over the remains at twilight

holding onto life for you

while you are swept into

the timeless ocean.

REQUIEM AT CHRISTMASTIME

I stood before the marble stone

amidst a curtain and blanket of white

while tinsel fell from the sky

and the stars shone like Christmas lights.

My eyes blurred and tears

rolled freely down my face

the warm liquid mixing

with the cold blanket which covered

your eternal bed encased.

I leaned on the stone headboard

and knelt down to give you one last kiss

goodnight,

but there was no warmth, nor breath,

only my tears melting into your bed of white.

~

For my father, Alfonso, who died in 1976. In my dream I visited his grave at Christmas and wrote this poem.

A MI PADRE

Tristísimo panteón

Yo te saludo

Y a ti me acerco

Sin temor ni espanto.

Vengo a regar

Con mi copioso llanto

La tumba de mi padre

Que aquí encuentro.

Permite que me acerque

a esa morada

Lóbrega y desierta

Para decir,

para decir

A mi padre adorado

"¡Padre, despierta!

¡Que tu hija aquí se halla!"

Cuan dichoso padre mío

Tendiste el raudo vuelo

Y te remontaste al cielo

Donde habita el Creador;

Mientras que yo caminando

Por este mundo desierto

Vengo con paso incierto

A colocarte una Flor...

∼

This is a poem for my father. I dreamt this poem in Spanish a year after he died. At the time, I didn't even know what some of the words meant. I won an award for this poem in 1977.

English translation follows.

A MI PADRE (ENGLISH TRANSLATION)

Mournful grave,

I greet you,

And I approach you

Without fear or dread.

I come to water,

With my copious tears,

My father's grave,

Which I find here.

Allow me to approach

That dwelling place,

Gloomy and deserted,

To say,

To say

To my beloved father,

"Father, wake!

Your daughter is here!"

How joyfully, my father,

You took swift flight

And rose to heaven

Where the Creator dwells.

While I walk

Through this deserted world

With uncertain steps

To place a flower on your grave.

ROMEO AND JULIET

Thousands of miles away

safe in my American kitchen

while the birds sing

and my coffee gets cold

I weep over the news

describing your death.

Run to freedom

to be slaughtered,

two lovers of different beliefs

come together to love and die

before you live.

Between heaven and hell

you lie on the cold ground

in an eternal embrace while

war rages hot over your cold bodies.

No one dares touch you,

six days of timeless conflict.

On the seventh day you are buried,

as the guns continue

roaring red anger

between your people.

∼

Honouring those who die in senseless wars still loving what is left of our humanity.

SHADOWS BEFORE SPRING

Have you ever been so

lonely

you could hear your heartbeat

echo against the silent walls of your

life,

vacant spaces where

there should be laughter and

joy,

when the song of the swallows

gleefully nesting under eaves

annoys instead of embraces.

This aloneness with no words,

your heart cracked open

like glass shattering on

stone

fragments spraying out

into a dark world,

a world you used to

love.

Loneliness is more than being

alone,

it is the vacant stare in your

eyes,

It is the cry that catches in your

throat,

the mechanical way you pet your

dog

that no longer comforts.

When the sun ceases to

warm,

and the breeze no longer

inspires,

when you've lost the salty taste of the

ocean

replaced by the grit of sand in your

mouth.

You have volunteered for this,

registering at the local grocery
store
when the peaches were too
ripe
and the cantaloupe
tasteless,
when you forgot you had no
change
for the man begging outside the
door
swamped in his own
darkness.
Do you know this loneliness?
I do. I will. I have
gone into the shadows for a bit
to rest my soul in its
aloneness,
armed only with the belief that
I will rise from my
Hades
like Persephone waiting
for the flowers to
bloom.

WAITING

I'm tired of waiting-

Waiting for things to get better

Waiting for sun

or rain

Waiting for the right guy

Waiting to belong

Waiting until I'm older or wiser while wishing I was

younger and blissfully ignorant

Waiting for the stars on a cloudy night

Waiting to fill my bucket list

Waiting to lose 5 pounds before I eat a whole pizza

Waiting for summer to eat ice cream

Waiting for shooting stars

Waiting for the right client, project or career

Waiting to be inspired

Waiting to be loved and cared for

Waiting for permission

Waiting for someone to buy me flowers

Waiting to feel strong enough to climb cliffs or kayak the ocean

Waiting to retire

Waiting for the writing muse

I'm tired of waiting for things that may never arrive

I'm just so fucking tired of waiting

When I'm able to do all of it

For myself

How I want

When I want

Right now

ALL THE THINGS

Had I known how this would end

I would've held you a few moments longer.

I would've smiled more, held hands on morning walks.

I would've listened to your silence deeply.

If I'd known how this would end

I would've chosen you over and over again, always.

I would've been braver when we were both afraid.

I would've prioritised peace and joy and love

Over career, money and prestige.

If I'd known how this would end

I would've dared more, shared adventures with abandon,

Spoken loving words daily, whispered dreams in the moonlight.

All the things I would've done differently

I say at night when no one listens.

Haunting memories I can't escape.

Time is a trickster, deceiving us

Telling us that moments don't count,

that all that matters

Is future or past,

Success and significance,

A magician disappearing me into my longing

Fighting to wrestle each lost moment back into my life.

If only I'd known how this would end

How different they would be,

All the things.

WHISPERS IN THE WALLS

I lose my words now when I speak,

they hide behind old doorways

and slip into the crevices in the walls.

Once when I tried to catch them

they ran out with the cat

fleeing into the garden to burrow

in the fallen leaves now brown

from their graves in damp earth.

We used to be friends,

I call out, hoping they remember,

hoping I remember

the term for tired, for grief,

for longing.

Once so elegant we danced together

forming stories, poems and ideas;

we are becoming strangers and

it hurts to see them leave me

without as much as a glance back.

WHITE HARBOR

Sitting on the pier

While the cold north wind

Blows

Thoughts and memories

Through

And past me,

Thinking of times that once were

And people once mine

Wondering all the while

What happened

To that fleeting gold star

Called Time.

Wishing I could catch

The clouds in my hands

Embrace

Memories in my mind

To reach the soaring seagulls

Calling to me echoes of the past

In their distant whine.

Letting me sail on their wings

Skipping over the white-capped waves

Of time

To grasp something

Beyond the blue

horizon.

I DIED A THOUSAND DEATHS

You cannot love a corpse

whose eyes have been sealed,

whose skin has been seared black

exposing the fragile bones

that did not burn

in the fire of life,

whose blood became

the river on which love floated

carried to a lifeless sea

that not even the albatross

dares cross.

SEDUCTION

You didn't know what I was thinking,

neither did I.

A compelling need

to change,

to save my life.

Success

wears like a mask

and behind the mask

a liar,

a traitor to my Maker,

to my soul,

to my essence.

Seduced.

WHEN I DIE

And when I die

you will mourn a stranger

unless you loved me

enough

to see me for who

I am.

Scatter my ashes to

the wind.

My soul

will paint a rainbow

for you.

Look for the sundog

to know I have been set free.

A BEAR IN THE FOREST

Soft brown moccasins walk the

muddy path

littered with dying leaves

crinkle and crack

under the weight

of the dark-skinned woman.

A bear roars in the forest.

Do trees hear?

BATTERED

You beat me for every word I say,

like every-day china I am chipped

and broken into pieces

by blows and words.

I cry for all

of me

beaten and broken

women children

flesh, bone, blood

exposed.

Words,

disguised as truths

protect you

man woman

husband wife

owner property

Tomorrow,

they will find me

broken into jagged pieces,

bloody remnants of woman

flesh, bone, blood

carried out and

buried

anonymously,

word by word.

CONTEXT

It was out of context

my life

the awesome machinations

of the father world

they told me I belonged

pieces of me in neat little

packages

assembly line feelings

riding old grey conveyer belts

emptying into dark holes

for storage somewhere

FEAR OF FALLING

A hollow emptiness in

the pit of my stomach

grows large

as the ground removes

itself.

Arms flailing,

heart beating madly,

legs sprawled,

I fall deeper and deeper

until in midair I

learn to fly and float

on the thermals in

the canyon.

Such freedom I have

not known.

From fear comes freedom.

I fly like the eagle

having conquered my

fear of falling.

MEMORIES

She wears the bracelet like a

coat keeps you warm in winter.

Her blue shirt cuff exposes one charm,

then another, as the sleeve rolls over

her freckled arm.

Dinner with a ghost, a bottle of red wine

the first course.

Absentmindedly she

allows her slender, manicured fingers to

caress each charm as if rubbing them

the genie would grant her wishes.

Memories strung on sterling, each bead a moment

in time linking past to present.

"Paris was wonderful in the fifties", she says.

Dinner in Boston tonight

while she dines in Paris 1956.

SONG FOR OPHELIA

She is alone.

She is always alone.

She watches autumn escape

in crayon colors

burnt umber sienna goldenrod

through warm breath peepholes

on frosty window panes.

Ophelia sits in an old oak rocking chair

rock rock

with quilted memories covering her lap,

grandma's shawl around brittle shoulders

rock rock back and forth

like the tick tock of time passing

on the pendulum face of grandfather clock.

Ophelia hums a song she remembers in tune to the tick tock

tick tock rock rock

wonders as it rains

burnt umber sienna goldenrod

where time has gone

sees in the cloudy pane a reflection of a woman

her skin wrinkled and cracking

like autumn leaves saved under glass

as youth floats past on the breeze

Ophelia hums a song

tick tock rock rock.

THE LATINA WASHES HER FACE

hunched over a sink too low for my gaze to wrap around

the mirror with patches of unglued advertisements that say do not remove

once upon a time

I wore another face

red kerchief encircles head

keeps hair out of eyes, big eyes,

remove black leftover eyeliner

now can I really see?

deep dirt in pretty pores dig it out with green, minty suds

water smells like sewer as it slinks down the drain

see what is so

no more makeup

clean Noxema skin but dark not white

eyes blink back the suds wash away god's grime

that scrubbed fresh feeling

but the red cowboy kerchief got wet

HORMONES

Raging hormones they say.

The earth shakes and I am still.

AT&T reaches out and touches someone,

me,

and I cry mush tears for no reason at all.

The sun sets over the horizon

and I am overcome,

mortified in public that I should

spill emotion all over the pier.

I'm happy.

I'm sad.

I'm tired.

I'm afraid.

All at once.

Raging hormones
play me like a marionette.
I bounce up and down all day.
I tumble not knowing if I am
upright or upside down.
I am attacked on all sides,
a warrior in battle vying for
endocrinological victory.
I retreat.
I cry.
I advance.
I'm angry.
I escape.
I'm happy.
I surrender.

HISTORY ON THE WALL

Once the walls were stark white

and blank,

like empty canvas waiting to be imagined.

Messy fingerprints painted on railings,

ancient doorknobs dotting closed doors,

paint-spattered windowsills.

Walls now papered and framed

with stolen images and wishful illusions.

History recorded in Kodachrome

exposing all.

Life pours from ceiling to floor

filling spaces as if to

beat death at the races.

History on the wall.

Life in my pocket.

MOVING

I store my life in boxes

tied up in neat knots,

waiting to be shipped away from now

into an unsure future.

I weep over the memories of the work,

the life, the letters,

so telling of who I was,

a foundation of who I will be.

The unknown is frightening.

MOVING II

If I make enough lists,

if I do enough work,

if I don't stop,

if I don't listen,

if I keep talking,

if I resist the letters,

if I don't look at the pictures,

if I don't stop,

I won't feel the sadness

of letting go.

I won't cry.

THE MYSTERY

We take the hand of

darkness.

Feed the head

foolish food while

the heart

starves.

Pyramids-

hot stone cones of

cold death-

tomb of Pharaohs-

such mystery.

MOVEMENT THREE
RETURNING

ON MYSTICISM

ON DREAMS

BIRTH OF THE MYSTIC

The world reveals itself to me

Eyes open

Honouring life

Blessings like rose petals

Float through the air

On my knees in gratitude

To the One.

I walk the bridge between the worlds

Going home

Hand in hand with God.

BELIEF

They say that God is everywhere

in everyone

in everything.

I say

God is in the morning dew,

in the laughter of children,

in the wrinkled hands of a grandmother,

in the scent of a rose.

God is in heartbreak

and in my lover's embrace.

God waits at the burial mound

and stands beside the mother giving birth.

One day we will meet

hands extended

welcoming me like

the child who had been lost,

now home.

GOD IS PRAYING TONIGHT

I think God is praying tonight.

There's something

about the way the wind is blowing,

the twinkling of the stars

and the way the palm tree fronds

dance in the breeze.

There is music.

The creatures of the night are singing.

In between the notes the universe speaks.

In the silent moments between the wind blowing,

the creatures singing

and the palm trees dancing

I feel the entire universe

as one symphony of light and sound and silence

harmonising its sonata.

It's not dark.

It's not light.

Each takes its turn on the universal dance floor.

I think God is praying tonight.

I must listen.

∼

I wrote this poem about my experience one night in the Ecuadorian rainforest. It was an experience of Oneness with All, my lived experience of the shamanic principle of Unidad / Totalidad.

INVITATION TO DINE

God invited me to her table

to dine with the angels

in a light blue room

filled with harps and music

which float like stars in a

deep, dark, blue sky

savouring every succulent morsel

of feast on my soul so

I know the taste of a tethered

star to my tongue

before it is digested

somewhere deep down

so I can use

energy to live life and

every succulent moment morsel

is savoured.

A HOLY MIST

The duality of change exists

in the moment when the past

becomes the future.

Where what was becomes a

different what will be.

The moment when the night greets the dawn,

on the horizon where the earth meets the sky.

At the point that rain becomes snow,

Consciousness arises like a mist on the waters.

THE DREAM: ACT VI

I saw them glide by me

in a nightmare I had last night.

They were the ghosts and images of times past

of people, of places, soaring in flight.

These visions appeared faded

in a fog or haze of light.

I was scared yet I reached out to grasp,

to comprehend the disturbing sight.

I felt tears stirring.

My eyes moistened. I think I cried.

I was caught in a warp of emotion and nostalgia.

I had thought the essence of me had died.

I floated aimlessly

through the vastness of a dark, forbidding sky.

There was no path. There was no road.

A distant, glowing star, my only guide.

On this celestial stage life was presented,

acted, yes, dramatised.

They chanted. They laughed. They wept.

Scenes from chapters forgotten before my eyes.

I was spectator.

I was actor, then victim all in one.

A wail, a scream, a curtain of darkness.

I opened my eyes and life's play was done.

When I awakened I realised

it was merely a dream I had been shown.

And all that remained on that mythical stage

was a shadow left standing alone.

MY QUEST

I come upon the crossroad

I hesitate in flight

the path of truth I'm shown

seeking guidance in the light.

The Quest bids me move forward

fear stops me in my tracks

my feet decide which way to go

there is not going back.

Courage seeps out of me

I struggle to keep a hold

the road is long and dark to see

"You will be wounded," I am told.

As I gaze into my heart

and call to my Knowing

the Voice tells me I cannot part
there are others following.
I come here seeking freedom
my spirit must now soar.
I take my sword, fight the demon
at the threshold of life's door.

My story is old and yet new
there have been those chosen few
who began the journey so long ago
in whose footsteps I now follow.
Peace be with you and with me
a blessing come from all Three.
To you I pray, grant me grace
that soon I will look upon the face
of Truth, Love and Harmony
for all of Eternity.

SHAMAN'S CEREMONY

In the firelight

painted bodies writhing,

chanting, bleeding

soul into the night -

the dance of the dead.

Through slivers of dream light

and smoky mists I see images of

ancient times and hear

voices mixed with rattle,

the cadence of drums

keeping time with

the heartbeat of the night.

Masked shaman

anoints ecstatic initiates.

I fall to my knees

surrendering myself to

the ceremony.

My own life

lived to died to lived again.

Redemption.

SLEEPWALKER

Childhood memories of

moist, sweet grass cut

on Sunday mornings,

the omnipresent toll

of the local church bell,

amazing, winged fairies

drinking dew drop prisms

reflecting

brilliant sun diamonds.

Memory moments

strung like pearls around

my heart.

Sleepwalker

awaken,

rise on child wings,

take flight with the fairies.

SCULPTING THE SOUL

They told me to sculpt a most beautiful statue

to embody the soul in marble and pearl.

The stone so smooth and rippled with earth

colours so lovely so worthy of her.

I bent forward and kissed it

then picked up the knife.

I made the first stroke

bringing marble to life.

A bit here and a bit there

she began to take shape.

The days passed so quickly

I toiled and they wait.

Came the day of unveiling

much fanfare and glee.

The music and crowds

all had arrived to see.

For the soul under canvas

the moment did loom.

The veil was lifted,

silence hushed the room.

There in the space

once hidden from view

where stood the marble

with earthen hue

were silence and emptiness

the soul laid bare-

neither carved nor created,

pure essence, a sacred prayer.

GLIMPSES OF POEMS

Those fleeting glimpses of poems

that dart before my eyes

while I stare into headlights

or watch shower drops

wet brown skin.

Words in my ears

rambling voices

like so many broken records

tangled tape

scenes appear

disappear

into the twilight of my conscious

unconscious.

I reach out quickly to

grab them.

They evaporate into still air

without a memory trace.

Not even in my sleep

can I recall their shadows

long enough to capture them

in pretty jars.

CHANCE

I take a chance

every time I show you my poems.

A chance that you will think

that this is dumb,

or I am insane,

or somehow not good enough.

Don't compare me to the masters.

I am a newcomer.

My vulnerability shows

like a pair of unzipped pants

my "fly" is open and

I'm afraid hurt will

creep in.

Standing in empty space,

fingers pointing,

paper poem waving like

a flag in parade,

I feel small.

I am wounded and

willing to show you

so that you may

learn from the

story I tell

in my poem.

THE PLACE OF WORDS

It's not enough to visit

that place of words

where

synonyms and antonyms play games

where images can be touched through sounds and pauses

and vowels and consonants come alive.

I want to live there.

THE SILENT ONES

The silent ones

Walk softly on the earth

Between the spaces of our lives

Leaving droplets of wisdom

In a silent gaze

That shifts everything.

The silent ones

Lay no claim to goodness

Do not seek fame or limelight

Dissolve into the evening starlight

Without a word or wave

No need to say farewell.

The silent ones

Change everything yet are unseen

Pulse to the universal rhythm

Outside of human drama and noise

Dropping love petals in their path

Gifts from another place.

The silent ones

Need not speak, or sing or write

A gaze, a silence, a tear

Love without measure

The language they speak

For those few that can understand.

The silent ones

Wait for the rising

Pray for the dawn

Hope for the awakening

Patiently doing their work

Unseen.

THE OCEAN I SOURCED FROM

I am reminded that gods are human

and humans are godly,

that the smallest child

may be my greatest teacher,

that life demands I climb the highest mountain

and invites me to sail the smoothest sea.

I am reminded that words may sing

and words may sting,

that the smoke from my hearth

smells of the scorching of our wars,

that the peace in silence

is known through the heartbeat of struggle.

I am reminded that clouds are keepers of dreams

and harbingers of storms,

that the icicles that frame my breath

are dissolved by my living,

that rainbows in their luminescence

are the markers of Nature's tears.

I am reminded that courage appears

only when fear is present,

that the day is known by its

marriage to the night

and my salty tears are borne of sorrow

as they are of joy.

I am reminded that the child I hold is ours

even as he dances away,

that the love I feel for you is infinite

and fleeting,

that forgiveness of others begins

with compassion for self.

I am reminded that the ocean I sourced from

patiently awaits my return.

BETWEEN ROOT AND SKY

In the womb of the world a seedling stirs,

wrapped in the warmth of the great mother,

cradled by the basket of all that is.

A vibration enters the earth,

a pulse becoming root, becoming stem,

stem to blossom, blossom to bark,

raising her limbs to the sky

defiantly declaring her place among all things.

A lifetime passes, a witness to stories of

peace, of war, of storms, of seasons imprinted

with loss, grief and longing.

No hurricane has felled her,

with roots as strong as anchors.

No tornado has broken her,

with limbs that learned to bend.

If not for her scars, her love could not flow to

a world hungry for mercy,

a sacred contract, bleeding beauty,

between root and sky,

a signpost to all that is holy.

NOTES

A sacred space for your thoughts and reflections.

ABOUT THE AUTHOR

Alicia M. Rodriguez is an award-winning Latina author of reflective nonfiction, memoir, and poetry exploring mindfulness, spirituality, personal growth, and conscious living.

Through lived experience and intimate storytelling, her work invites readers into presence, self-awareness, and meaning—especially during times of transition, grief, and inner transformation.

Known for a grounded, non-dogmatic voice, she blends contemplative insight with practical wisdom rather than prescriptive self-help.

Her award-winning memoir, *The Shaman's Wife: A Mystical Journey of Surrender and Self-Discovery*, details her transformative eight-year journey with an Ecuadorian shaman. Her work has been featured in numerous online publications, including the anthology, *Still, She Writes* and Thrive Global, Tiny Buddha, Writerly Magazine, Tiferet Journal, Substack, and Medium.

As a seasoned executive coach with over two decades of experience, Alicia has empowered thousands of individuals worldwide to connect with their hearts, spirit, and intelligence, creating powerful futures. She believes that we are spiritual beings having a human experience, a perspective that has taken her from corporate boardrooms to the rainforests, mountains, and coast of Ecuador.

Currently residing in the stunning Algarve region of Portugal, Alicia finds inspiration and joy in her morning cliff walks with her dog, Sophie. Her serene environment fuels her creativity, allowing her to continue enchanting audiences with her writing. Alicia also offers mentorship and private curated retreats in Portugal, empowering people to embrace limitless possibilities and forge powerful futures.

- instagram.com/msaliciamrodriguez
- facebook.com/MsAliciaMRodriguez
- aliciamrodriguez.substack.com
- linkedin.com/in/aliciamrodriguez
- amazon.com/author/aliciamrodriguez
- goodreads.com/aliciamrodriguez
- bsky.app/profile/aliciarod.bsky.social
- pinterest.com/AM_Rodriguez
- threads.com/@msaliciamrodriguez

FOLLOW ALICIA ON SOCIAL MEDIA

- Website: https://aliciamrodriguez.com/
- Instagram: https://www.instagram.com/msaliciamrodriguez/
- Substack: *Nothing Is Ordinary*: https://aliciamrodriguez.substack.com/
- Newsletter: https://alicia-m-rodriguez.kit.com/amrnewsletter
- Free Life Design Assessment Download: https://alicia-m-rodriguez.kit.com/lifedesignassessment
- Linktree: https://linktr.ee/aliciamrodriguez

SCAN THE QR CODE TO VISIT ALICIA'S WEBSITE

ALSO BY ALICIA M. RODRIGUEZ

Publications, Resources, Downloads

COMING SOON:

The Stillness Within: A Contemporary Mystic's Path to Reflection, Deep Connection and Authentic Living

THE END

If a poem here resonated or soothed, a review on Amazon or Goodreads helps these words find others who might need them. Thank you for taking the moment to share.

www.ingramcontent.com/pod-product-compliance
Lightning Source LLC
Chambersburg PA
CBHW032038290426
44110CB00012B/862